The Multipotentialite's Guide: Working from Home

Learn How to Effectively Work Remotely, Maintain Uninterrupted Focus, and Create a Space Where You Want to Work

By: Alex Sinatra

Notices

Mentions of specific companies, organizations, or authorities in this publication does not imply endorsement by the author or publisher, nor does mention of specific companies, organizations, or authorities imply that they endorse this publication, its author, or the publisher.

This publication is designed to provide accurate and authoritative information in regard to the subject matter covered. It is sold with the understanding that the author is not engaging in rendering legal advice, professional advice, or professional service of any kind. The author disclaims any and all liability to any party for any loss, damage, or disruption caused by errors, omissions, or taking advice from this book, whether such errors or omissions result from negligence, accident, or any other cause.

Dedication

Thank you to my friends and family for helping me through my work from home journey. Working from home is an adjustment for everyone in your life and my family has helped me set and maintain boundaries. I now get to spend more time with my family and friends and it has been a huge blessing for me. My father is an author and each time I sit down to write, he inspires me and his love motivates me. Check out his first novel, The Bone-Handled Stiletto, available on Amazon. My mother has shown me how to be graceful even during the stressful times of work from home, so thank you for your patience and kindness. Thank you Casey for editing this manuscript and teaching me something new every day. All glory to God, for without Him, none of this would be possible.

Table Of Contents

Preface: Meet the Author

First off, let me explain what a Multipotentialite is and why I consider myself one. Basically we are people with many different interests and creative pursuits in life. We have no "one true calling" in life the way specialists do. We have many paths and pursue all of them, either sequentially or simultaneously.

There are **3 superpowers** we possess:

1. **Idea synthesis**: Taking knowledge from different fields and merging them into a new idea

2. **Rapid learning**: Ability to go all-in on a subject and become well versed in it quickly

3. **Adaptability**: Ability to adapt to ideas, processes, and roles seamlessly

My background is in both **marketing**, I hold a BBA in Marketing from Texas A&M University Mays Business School, and **law**, I am licensed to practice law, and have practiced since 2014, and went to Texas A&M University School of Law. I consider myself a multipotentialite because I not only have a degree in marketing and a law license, but I was a competitive gymnast, a writer, an actress with an acting agent for 15 years, and more.

Because of this, I see problems, issues, and industries in a new way. That is why I decided to write a series of books helping others learn what I have over the years while also continuing to educate myself on new topics. I also started a podcast, Your Potential for Everything, that supplements these books and delves deeper into each topic with my guests, link in Chapter 9.

When an employer looks at my résumé they might see me as flighty, but that is truly not the case. If they asked I would tell them why I left certain companies (the cultural values didn't mesh or I refused to be part of unethical behavior or I was harassed) or why I have held multiple positions at once. This is the plight of the Multipotentialite. However, it can be a huge asset to companies who employ us.

I am at my best when I am able to problem solve issues from many different perspectives. If I am asked about a legal problem in the marketing department, it might lead me to solve the problem then come up with a whole new marketing scheme in an hour for the new campaign. If I walk past someone's desk and hear them talking about machine learning, then I will have a conversation with them about the various machine learning algorithms I have studied and their thoughts on data analytics in sports.

We are also known as renaissance men and women, but for some reason we have been seen in a negative light recently. Currently I have been working on many different areas:

- Starting a podcast
- Learning Italian from my cousin
- Focusing on my fitness
- Being a subject matter expert in meetings on networking
- Applying to marketing, PR, and legal roles
- Writing articles and creating videos for USA TODAY's NFL Wire Sites and Dallas Sports Fanatic

Those are just a few of the tasks I am currently interested in and working on for fun.

Multipotentialites might look like we don't know what we want to do, but that isn't the case. We have interests in a variety of fields and when those interests are allowed to be merged together, then we have a crazy amount of information and work to give to our companies and colleagues.

A few multipotentialites or renaissance men & women you might be familiar with:

- Leonardo Da Vinci
- Thomas Jefferson
- Benjamin Franklin
- René Descartes
- Isaac Newton
- Aristotle
- Maya Angelou
- Richard Branson
- Hedy Lamarr
- Beatrix Potter
- You?

Now that you have a little background on me and what the heck a multipotentialite is, let's get to work on teaching you How To Work From Home!

Chapter 1: Introduction

This is the second book in The Multipotentialite's Guide series. If you are interested in learning about Networking in the Virtual Age: Learn How to Network, Make Lasting Connections, and Land a Job In the Digital Age, then check out my first book in the series available on Amazon, linked below in Chapter 9.

Working From Home isn't a new concept, stay-at-home moms and dads have been doing it for millennia. It is an art form, however, and one that some people are still learning at a finger-painting pace. You want to be the Michelangelo of working from home, not a macaroni stuck to construction paper kind of artist.

Many businesses don't train their employees how to work from home. This may be the reason so many employers have been reluctant to allow working from home. I also want to clarify that when I say working from home, I also include the ability to work remotely or work from anywhere into that mix. With the numerous technological advances coming out, it is possible to have a work from anywhere status as opposed to just working from home.

I have been known to work from foreign countries and beaches when I was working fully remote and ultimately it doesn't matter if you are at home or in the forest as long as you have wifi and are getting your work done on time. So remember when I say work from home, I truly mean remote work or working from anywhere.

It is more vital than ever now to learn how to work from home because it is a valuable skillset for your professional arsenal. According to an MIT survey[1] of 25,000 American workers in early April of 2020 found that, "34% of those who'd been employed four weeks earlier said they're currently working from home. Combined with the roughly 15% who said they'd been working from home pre-COVID-19, that means nearly half the U.S. workforce might now be remote workers. And that's also true, the researchers say, for workers 55 and older."

But why should you listen to me about working from home? What makes me so special?

I have worked from home in some capacity since 2016 and have held a fully remote job at USA TODAY Sports Media Group's NFL Wire sites (say that ten times fast). My experiences and suggestions come from years of mastering the art of working from home along with harnessing knowledge from others who work from home. I am not claiming to be the Claude Monet of working from home, but maybe la less cool version of Banksy.

I have also held jobs that weren't fully remote, but allowed me the flexibility to work from home when I needed it. I have the experience working fully remote and partially remote jobs and have learned to do both efficiently and effectively.

In any event, having the knowledge of how to effectively work from home can make you a thought

---

[1] https://adobe.ly/2ODpl2x

leader on the topic. That could lead to more work from home opportunities for you or even have you be the go-to person at your job on working from home. While it doesn't take much to go from finger-painting to paint-by-numbers to Banksy status, the transformation can make all the difference for you.

Chapter 2: Why Should I Learn to Work From Home?

A recent article from Forbes[2] asked an important question, *Is Working From Home The Future Of Work?*

I truly believe that the COVID-19 pandemic has forever changed the way we will work post-pandemic. Many businesses are understanding the value of allowing employees to work from home. Employees who understand the ins and outs of working from home are also realizing how valuable it is to have this flexibility.

But not everyone has the luxury of being able to work from home. Jobs that are done mostly on a computer or through phone calls can easily adjust to at-home working, but manual labor jobs like servers, doctors, and construction workers are harder or even impossible to make virtual.

A Pew research study[3] shows that, "Around a quarter (24%) of workers in "management, business and financial" occupations – such as corporate executives, IT managers, financial analysts, accountants and insurance underwriters – have access to telework. So do 14% of "professional and related" workers, such as lawyers, software designers, scientists and engineers."

Larger employers are also more likely to allow working from home than smaller employers. Regional variations

---

[2] https://bit.ly/2ZI1PHZ

[3] https://pewrsr.ch/3fEoKJM

aren't too staggering with between 6%-8% of workers having access to telework and it rises slightly in New England where the number is 11%. However, unsurprisingly, the numbers are higher in other countries.

In Scandinavian countries[4] the numbers are higher for telework. In Sweden, about 20% of all gainfully employed are teleworking. A 2017 study[5] of 30 European countries found that 23% of Danes, 21% of Dutch, and 18% of Swedes worked from home "at least several times a month." The lowest work-from-home rates in the study were in Bulgaria and Cyprus and are on par with the U.S.

According to a recent Forbes article[6], working from home can: boost your productivity, improve your work/life balance, and foster better mental health. It is also a more sustainable option that helps reduce pollution from commuting. Now working from home might not magically be something your employer will allow you to do 100% of the time. However, employers are starting to understand the value of working from home and if you are skilled at working remotely, you might be able to negotiate more flexibility into your job.

Worker productivity has skyrocketed recently despite the COVID-19 pandemic sweeping the globe which

---

[4] https://onlinelibrary.wiley.com/doi/abs/10.1111/ntwe.12060

[5] https://journals.sagepub.com/doi/full/10.1177/0001699317722593

[6] https://bit.ly/2Zl1PHZ

has forced many to work in new ways. Prodoscore, a leader in employee visibility software, released reports that indicated worker productivity is up in 2020 by 47%[7]. The company also evaluated around 100 million data points from 30,000 U.S.- based Prodoscore users during March and April of 2020 and compared them to date in a compared timeframe in 2019.

The findings were quite interesting:

- Telephone calling up 230%
- Customer Relationship Management system activity up 176%
- Email activity up 57%
- Chat messages up 9%

The data also showed some helpful statistics on when people were most productive:

- The average worker starts work at 8.32 a.m. and ends work at 5.38 p.m.
- Tuesday, Wednesday, and Thursday are the most productive days, in that order
- Friday is the least productive day, followed by Monday
- The most productive period during the workday is from 10.30 a.m. to 3.00 p.m.
- Employee "ramp-up" to being productive takes one to three hours daily

This information can help you understand how average people work and you can schedule your tasks based

---

[7] https://www.businesswire.com/news/home/20200519005295/en/

around these most productive timeframes. Scheduling calls outside of the 10.30 a.m. - 3.00 p.m. window can help you utilize less productive time in an efficient way. Starting with simple, throw-away tasks during the 1-3 hour ramp-up period can ease your brain into productivity. However, you have to find what works best for you and your life and schedule.

Twitter recently announced[8] their employees can work from home forever even after offices open back up after the COVID-19 pandemic. Google extended its work from home orders until July 2021, Facebook expects to have half its workforce remotely working in 5-10 years, and both Amazon and Apple are having their employees work from home for the rest of 2020.

If you have the skills to work from home then you will be an even more valuable asset to big and small companies alike. While work from home might not be something companies do 100% of the time, it is an option more companies will be affording their employees who are able to do it well. Perhaps working remotely will be incorporated into your company a few times a week or on an as-needed basis. In any event, having the skills to be effective and efficient at it will only serve you well.

---

[8] https://cnb.cx/3i2CLSj

Chapter 3: Get Hygge with It

A great work space is key to effectively working from home. There is a word in Danish called hygge pronounced (/ˈh(y)o͞ogə,ˈho͞ogə/). There isn't a translation of the word into English per se, but essentially it is a feeling of coziness that engenders a feeling of comfort and well-being. This should be the basis of how you want your workspace to feel, but be careful because too much hygge and you will be falling asleep and missing those pertinent work calls.

Let's go over a checklist of what makes a space hygge and then translate that into workspace hygge. My book club, *The Book Club for Professional Who Don't Read Good*, read the book *The Year of Living Danishly* by Helen Russell. She outlines what Danes do to create this feeling of hygge. There is a correlation to how your space looks to how you feel in your space.

- **Lighting.** A big component to creating a space where you want to be is appropriate lighting. Having a lamp that is too bright or too dim can affect the way you feel. For instance, I have never heard someone say they loved the feeling of neon office lights, because frankly that light is too abrasive for any occasion. It is essential to have lighting that is appropriate for the room and to try to incorporate as much natural light as possible. Work-related headaches can sometimes be remedied by proper lighting in your space and a good pair of blue-light blocking glasses

- **Quality Furniture.** Good design makes people happy. I am not advocating going out and replacing all your furniture, but rather making sure a few key pieces are quality. For instance, getting a desk chair that doesn't make your legs go numb is a good start. Too often people suffer through a bad chair with no lower back support and wonder why they have to see their chiropractor twice a week. Speaking of which I both need a new home office chair and a good adjustment. Do as I say, not as I do.

- **Neutral Colors.** You want a space where your mind isn't distracted by the decor. Having bold patterns and colors can sometimes distract the mind and the last thing you need during working from home is more distraction.

- **Banish Clutter.** Having clutter in your spaces subconsciously causes anxiety for some. Whether this applies to you or not, making sure your space is organized and clutter-free is huge. If the space is clutter-free you are going to be less distracted by the organizing you could be doing in the room.

- **Sound.** Creating a soothing playlist of nature or classical music can help you focus in your space and bring a peaceful quality.

- **Add Natural Elements.** Plants can add a sense of calm to a space and if you pick an easy plant that doesn't need much attention, then it won't feel like a chore to keep it alive.

Now that we are getting in the hygge mood and I can already feel you relaxing, let's talk about how this relates to your work space. These suggestions all still apply but their implementation will be a little different for a work space as opposed to a living space. These touches can work in a full-blown office or in a small window nook you turned into a workspace in your efficiency apartment.

Hygge in the Office

- **Lighting.** Whether you have the luxury of having a big desk for work or you are currently working on your lap, lighting is essential to creating a hygge environment. If you have the means to purchase new lighting fixtures for your office then be my guest, but make sure you go with soft lighting that illuminates your work space.

  However, a quick fix to your lighting woes is to change the lightbulbs in your space. I recently changed the lightbulb in my desk lamp and it completely transformed the space. I took a harsh bulb from my desk lamp and switched it to a softer glow that still lit up my work. I like to have a lot of light when I am working because it takes the strain off of my eyes, but I have never been a fan of the abrasive lights present in most offices. I am a light snob apparently.

  If you are able to work facing or near a window then opt for that as well. Natural light is always going to be better for working then electric or manmade light. Your eyes will thank you later. You can also opt for blue light blocking glasses if you stare at screens for long amounts of time. When I purchased my regular glasses I opted to pay a bit more for them to make them blue light blocking and I have noticed I have less headaches when I work long hours in front of the computer screen.

- **Quality furniture.** Quality doesn't always mean expensive so don't read past this part. What I mean by quality is a chair and desk that actually work together. You don't want a chair that is too tall for the desk so you have to sit sideways to get your legs under the desk. And on the opposite end you don't want a desk that is too tall for your chair. Studies have shown if you have a chair that helps you sit upright instead of slouching then you can have better mood and reduced stress[9]. It's science.

  Be sure the chair is comfortable as well and gives you good lower back support or you find a cushion to place behind your back that supports your lower back. Quality doesn't mean expensive, but rather it is something you feel comfortable sitting in for long stretches of time. Remember to take care of your body by using furniture that supports it properly. I prefer ergonomically designed chairs that help my lower back feel supported and not strained.

- **Neutral colors.** Different colors illicit different thoughts in people's minds. While there are individuals who promote one color over the other, you should ultimately place items in your work space that bring you happiness. I have found that I appreciate neutral colors in my work space because they don't distract me from my work.

---

[9] https://psycnet.apa.org/record/2014-37739-001

Busy patterns and bright patterns distract me from my work, but those patterns might be just what you need in your space.

You need to pick colors and items you place in your office that elicit the right feelings for you to do good work. You need to feel comfortable in the space you are in and that's where the design element comes into play.

- **Banish clutter.** Some people are able to work through mounds of clutter and they are productive and happy. For the rest of us, clutter is a distraction. When a space is cluttered it tends to have a negative effect on your work. You want to clean the clutter instead of read that work spreadsheet, however, if you walk into your work space every morning and it looks neat and tidy, it feels like you have already been productive without doing one task on your To Do list.

You want to be sure to have a work space that you are able to spread out on if that is your work style. I prefer to keep all my items in one area and work in a compartmentalized way. For me, I am extremely minimalist in the items I have on my desk. It makes me happy to have my desk neat and tidy with no clutter.

- **Sound.** It is so easy to be distracted by sound and in order to drown out those distracting sounds, it is best to add pleasing and relaxing sounds to your workspace. I prefer to listen to either classical music or nature sounds that are quiet but noticeable.

On the Headspace app, they have tracks of sounds that are called focus music. They are tones that elicit happy or calm feelings while not being distracting. Personally I pop on the Deep Blue track and go to work. I also add nature sounds into the mix when I am feeling a little restless indoors.

They also recently partnered with John Legend to create some focus music compilations, so definitely check out what they have to offer. And the last time I checked, they are offering free memberships for the unemployed.

- **Add Natural Elements.** It has been proven that plants make us happy. Having a small plant in your office space will make it a happier and more calming place to be. Succulents are pretty easy to take care of and work well in most spaces.

    The best plants for a home office include: Snake plant, African violet, English ivy, ZZ plant, Aloe, Philodendron, Tillandsia, Oxalis, Rex begonia, and Lucky bamboo.

    Plants also clean the air and for me, make me feel like I am not alone in my office because I have a beautiful living thing growing next to me.

- **Taking Breaks.** Be sure to take a break and enjoy some coffee or tea during the work day and actually leave your office space. This creates a sense of freedom that makes you feel great when you walk back into your space.

- **Get comfy.** Be sure you have a soft blanket nearby in case you want to wrap up your legs and get comfortable. I keep a nice powder pink blanket next to me and constantly pull it on or off depending on the temperature. Investing in a nice pair of fuzzy socks also puts you in the hygge mood and keeps you from being distracted by feelings of cold.

- **Be prepared.** You want to have all the items you need to work close by you so that you don't have to keep getting up to grab your notebook, a pen, or the phone number for IT. Be sure to have all the items you need up on the wall or on your desk so you don't have to leave your hygge office to search for an item.

- **Put on real clothes.** This doesn't mean you have to dress up in a suit and tie, but it does mean you shouldn't be in your pajamas. Looking the part during work from home helps to set your brain and psyche in the right place to work efficiently and precisely. Also, don't work from your bed if you can help it, it is bad for your back and can subconsciously confuse you into thinking the bed is for working and not for sleeping.

3 Expensive Ways to Hygge

1. Purchase an ergonomic new desk chair
2. Invest in custom lighting for your space
3. Purchase new desk that fits your new chair and your space

5 Inexpensive Ways to Hygge

1. Add a good desk lamp that lights your work space & change bulbs in overhead and desk lighting to soft lighting
2. Wear comfortable/warm socks and keep a ceiling fan or desk fan blowing
3. Add a sustainable yet deliciously scented candle to your workspace
4. Take scheduled coffee or tea breaks during the work day where you leave your office space
5. Have a comfy blanket or throw handy to cuddle up with in your chair

Chapter 4: The Benefits of Working From Home

In the Summer 2020 issue of Millie magazine[10], a financial magazine centered around women, there was an article entitled The Future of Work. It specifically mentioned that the COVID-19 pandemic may forever change the workplace for women. I believe it will change the workplace for everyone and women will especially benefit. Which is good news, because women still only make about $0.82 for every dollar men make with Black women and other women of color making far less than their Caucasian counterparts.

According to Millie magazine, nearly three quarters of CEOs anticipate that at least some fo their workers will move to permanent remote positions. Stephanie Nadi Olson the CEO of We Are Rosie states, "There's going to be a movement toward innovating and modernizing the way work happens. The companies that aren't doing it [remote work] are not going to be able to attract and retain talent."

Allowing remote work will make the workplace more inclusive by allowing those who were unable to join the traditional workforce due to home commitments or sickness, a chance to get back into the workforce. Many women have had to quit their jobs to raise a family and now with the rise of remote work, these

---

[10] https://www.realsimple.com/search?q=work%20from%20home

workers might be able to reenter the workforce and kick butt in the virtual boardrooms.

A 2019 survey by Zapier[11], a global remote company, cited that 62% of women and 53% of men want to work remotely. This was before the 2020 pandemic ever hit.

However, 40% of women and 25% of men say they don't work remotely because their company doesn't allow it. Knowledge workers, 66%, believe that by 2030 the physical office will be obsolete. The numbers are even more staggering amongst younger generations with 71% of millennials believing remote work will take over from a traditional office.

One major benefit of remote working is the flexibility it affords. You are able to work from the comfort of your home while taking your dog out for a walk or giving your baby a bath. You can easily walk to the kitchen for a snack when you feel the midday slump arising. If you get tired of one chair you can move to another. This ability to have a flexible schedule by remote working affords a better work life balance and integration which helps take the pressure off trying to fit all responsibilities into a single day.

The lack of commute is something I absolutely love and others have expressed similar thoughts. For those of us who have crazy traffic to and from work, you could easily waste three hours each day sitting in traffic and having your blood pressure spike through the roof. Not to mention the amount of money you

---

[11] https://zapier.com/blog/remote-work-report-by-zapier/

might be spending in gas and tolls. Time and cost savings are huge benefits when you get to have a 60 second commute to your home office. One of my friends who works fully remote, walks every morning as part of her morning routine and she describes those steps as her morning commute.

You also get to know your coworkers better. According to Diana Vienne of Notion Consulting, "People used to be ashamed to talk about personal commitments that interfered with work." Now, however, there are toddlers and pets crashing Zoom meetings and when leaders are showing this human side of themselves, they are gaining trust and loyalty from their employees.

Remote work is also great for self starters because they are able to work in an environment where they prioritize their own days and show what they are able to do when left to their own devices.

And if you aren't convinced about the benefits of remote work then take a look at this statistic from Zapier's study. "Full-time remote knowledge workers typically spend more hours, on average, each workday doing meaningful work (i.e., work that has significance and purpose) compared to their office worker counterparts. That's 6.2 hours for remote workers compared to 5.7 hours for office-bound ones."

There are pitfalls of remote work and for some, these challenges may not be worth the flexibility. However, remote work has been a game changer for me and my friends who have the option of remote work. We don't want to go back to the traditional office life.

Chapter 5: The Pitfalls of Working From Home

Remote work isn't all cherry gumdrops and scented roses. Did I say how bad I am at colloquial phrases? In any event, there are some pitfalls to working from home and these are sometimes too great for some people to want to overcome. Working from home isn't for everyone, but everyone can learn to be better at working from home.

Some of the most common pitfalls of working from home are constant distractions, communication issues, and loneliness. If you live in a house with anyone else whether family members, roommates, or even pets, there will always be physical distractions you must overcome or learn to live with in harmony.

If you aren't a self-starter then working from home might not come as naturally for you as it does for others. The same can be said if you are an extroverted person and love being around other people constantly. I often hear people say that working from home is hard for them because they feel extremely unproductive. This unproductiveness, however, could be because there isn't a time where the person plans their day out ahead of time and prepares for the remote work life. Working from home sometimes take a lot more intentionality than working from the office.

Communication is also an area where I hear people having trouble with when they transition from working in a traditional environment to the more flexible remote life. Maintaining good communication with your coworkers is key, but setting boundaries is also important. It is also extremely hard to read your coworkers via email, zoom, phone call, or text message. In days gone by you were able to read an email and walk to your coworkers office to gauge their actual intent, but now it is slightly more difficult to actually read whether that coworker was being passive aggressive in their email or not.

Another major pitfall of working from home, whether you are surrounded by roommates or not, is the feeling of being lonely. A report from Buffer showed the truth about the problems with remote work[12]. They asked 2,500 remote workers to talk about the benefits and struggles of working from home. The highest percentage of respondents indicated that unplugging after work, 22%, was their hardest struggle. They also reported loneliness at 19%.

Amir Salihefendic is the CEO of Doist, a company that inspires the workplace of the future by creating simple yet powerful productivity tools that promote a more balanced way to work and live. After seeing the statistics from the Buffer report, he said "remote work isn't just a different way to work – it's a different way to live. And, unlike what you might see on Instagram, working remotely doesn't mean you jet set to exotic locations to drink piña coladas on the beach." He continued and said "we need to acknowledge that isolation, anxiety, and depression are significant problems when working remotely, and we must figure out ways and systems to resolve these complex issues."

---

[12] https://buffer.com/state-of-remote-work-2019

A recent 2019 Forbes article[13] had an interesting quote from Dr. Amy Cirbus, PhD, LMHC, LPC, and Manager of Clinical Quality at Talkspace. She said, "Remote workers often experience symptoms of anxiety and depression at a higher rate than people commuting into traditional office spaces. Specifically, they report feelings of isolation and loneliness and high rates of worry about job performance and stability. Insomnia and sleep disturbance are common, along with increased fatigue, irritation, sadness and feelings of disconnection. Remote workers report a lack of concentration and focus that can compound and exacerbate these mental health challenges. It can lead to a loss of self-worth and a questioning of one's abilities. Combined together, these symptoms can have a significant impact on job performance, job satisfaction, and the efficiency of productive work."

How does this make sense? So many people seem to want to work from home due to increased flexibility. The results are interesting and actually make a lot of sense to me, when you dig into them, based on my own experiences and the experiences others have shared with me.

- More freedom and autonomy also requires managing tasks that possibly aren't your best skillset like IT troubleshooting, time management, and task prioritization.

- No ability to physically move up in an office like moving from a small cubicle into a larger corner

---

[13] https://bit.ly/3gY4PGr

office sometimes prevents workers from recognizing progress and achievements and sometimes they are overlooked for career development opportunities. If left unattended this can lead to a feel of stagnation or imposter syndrome.

- Sometimes you have to be in a constant state of hustle, especially if you are a freelancer and this can contribute to sustained stress.

- Sometimes remote workers forget to take breaks since there are no coworkers coming into their office or inviting them to grab lunch together. This lack of movement can cause ergonomic problems with the body and can result in an extremely sedentary lifestyle. If workers don't have good seating options then over time a worker's chin, shoulders, and back being in a compromised position can contribute to feelings of stress and depression.

- When workers are spread around the globe or around the country when working from home or otherwise, they can be informationally isolated. Perhaps a team member forgets to tell you about a task that needs completed that the boss told them in passing. This can compromise efficiency and cause feelings of worry about job performance, lack of team trust, questions about job security, and a lack of confidence.

Now that you know the pros and cons about working from home, let's turn to some tips and tricks to combat the negative issues and focus on what we can do to be the best version of our work from home selves.

Chapter 6: Tips & Tricks to Successfully Work From Home

There are many ways to be efficient and ultimately you have to find a mix that works for you. You might not be your most productive from 10 a.m. - 2 p.m. and that's okay, but you have to figure out your patterns and plan your schedule around those to optimize the flexibility of the work from home life.

On my podcast, **Your Potential for Everything**, four of my guests, in Series 2 episodes 5-8, discuss working from home and how they have done it efficiently and what has worked for them.

My friend Casey has been working from home since 2017 for a company based in the USA, while she is working and living in Thailand. She had to quickly adapt to a new way of working and a totally new culture. She has found some ways that work for her and allow her to be her most productive and efficient self. She shared some of these on the podcast, but I expounded upon them here.

- **Have a morning and evening routine.** In the mornings she is the most productive so she sets out to wake up early and utilize this time. She has a set morning routine that consists of not answering work or personal messages until about an hour after she has woken up. She has tea, breakfast, and lets out her cats. She sometimes even gets some steps in to start the morning on the right foot, no pun intended, which she calls her morning commute. She wants to incorporate meditations into her morning routine as well.

For me, I make sure to have a night routine as well since I find it hard to turn off my work brain at night. I start the routine about an hour and a half before my bedtime. Studies show you get your most restorative sleep from 10 p.m. - 2 a.m., so I try to be asleep by 10 p.m. I turn on soothing music, stop watching TV or Netflix, I light a candle, and wash my face and brush my teeth. By the time I lay down my body has realized that the next step is sleep.

Sometimes I can't fall asleep though because my brain is still racing. That's when I turn to headspace and their sleep series of sleepcasts, wind down meditations, nighttime SOS, sleep music, soundscapes, and sleep radio. To be honest, these sleep aids have been invaluable to me. Before implementing these sleep aids it would take me hours to fall asleep and wind down from work. Now I will sometimes fall asleep within 10-15 minutes of laying down.

Headspace also has work from home meditations to help you start your day and end your day. These are great for people who want to have a morning or evening routine, but don't know where to start.

Your morning and evening routine don't have to look like Casey's or mine, but routine is key in the work from home life. Since there is so much flexibility there is the pitfall of getting off task and not getting your work done. However, with a morning and evening routine you can be sure to prepare for the day in the morning and wind down from the workday in a way your body understands and then it will create a habit.

- **Communication is key.** Communication is always key in maintaining a stellar job performance, but it is even more critical while working from home. If you are a manager then be sure you are communicating clearly with your team and setting the expectations. When you are doing projects as an employee, be sure to check in with your boss and team periodically throughout the day to update them on work done. It is better to communicate more than you think is necessary than not communicating enough.

People report feeling lonely when they are working from home and this can stem from lack of communication with their colleagues and with their family or friends. When you work from home, you need to communicate at a greater frequency with your work colleagues. It keeps everyone on the same page. This communication doesn't have to be an hour-long Zoom session, but it can be a quick Slack message or a text message to check in with the group, your manager, or a colleague.

Recently, I heard some companies doing happy hours on Zoom and these consisted of discussing anything but work to keep that feeling of camaraderie amongst the team. They called them "water-cooler" moments and these are definitely important. Staying not only communicative, but also engaged is important for keeping the loneliness out of your work from home life.

Communication is also important with your family or those with whom you are living. Everyone needs to be on the same page about work and personal life. That brings me to my next point.

- **Set Boundaries.** Like in all aspects of your life both work and personal, you have to set boundaries. This is even more important when working from home. The tendency of our family and friends is to speak with us and interact with us when they see us. However, when you are working from home, this can become problematic and a detriment to your work.

You must set clear boundaries both physical and implied. If you have a particular space where you work then you need to inform family, friends, and roomies that when you are there you are working and are not to be disturbed unless there is a big issue. You can also place actual signs around you or on the doors to those rooms that indicate the same. I have a sign on two separate doors in big bold letters that indicate if the sign is up to text me if there is a problem.

You also must set boundaries that encompass time. For instance if you have to be on a call for a certain time, then communicating this multiple times will help everyone get on the same page. You must set these personal boundaries so everyone knows just because you are home, doesn't mean you are accessible.

This definitely works in an ideal world, but it won't work all the time and is more difficult with children at home. However, I have found that when you make guidelines like this into a game for kids, they are much more amenable to "playing the game."

The French call this boundary setting with kids the cadre, which loosely translates to frame or structure. Kids are allowed to have a lot of free rein within the structure, but must stay inside of it. For instance, if you are working and kids are in the house then you can make a rule that they can't come to your work room or area during a set time, but they can scream and yell or play with all their toys during that time as long as they don't come into your area. I am not necessarily advocating using your outside voice inside, but this is an example. Giving kids the ability to have freedom within a rigid structure can help with boundary setting in your work from home environment.

You must also set boundaries for your work colleagues. Some companies take advantage of those who are working from home and expect more work to be done and for people to be on call and answer their phones at all hours of the day and night. This shouldn't be the case and you must set up boundaries with your company, employees, colleagues etc. as soon as you can. If not, then you will be answering calls at midnight and not actually disconnecting from the job. This will lead to depression, anxiety, and a whole slew of mental health issues.

There are sometimes you must answer the phone or send the email outside of the framework you constructed and that is inevitable. However, making it clear to your work that you have a cutoff time and a particular start time along with a particular lunch time helps all involved. This step also involves great communication and constant reminders to those you work with of the boundaries. I have implemented boundaries at jobs and usually I wished I had set them up sooner, because surprisingly most people were respectful of those boundaries.

- **Utilize the Flexibility.** If you are working remotely or from home then you have some type of flexibility over your schedule. It is imperative that you use it to take full advantage of this new found freedom.

Casey has the ability to set her own schedule so she sets her work hours based upon her most productive times and takes breaks during her unproductive times. Not everyone has the ability to set their own schedule, but that doesn't mean you can't use the flexibility.

For me, I notice that Mondays and Fridays are the days I like to schedule meetings to keep my Tuesday - Thursday schedule open. Most people are more productive Tuesday - Thursday, according to studies, so I want to be sure I have those days open to work on any projects that other people might throw my way during the week. I use Mondays and Fridays for Zoom meetings and to get most of my work done since I know mid-week will probably be monopolized by other people's productivity peaking. I take the off hours at the law firm that other people don't like to take, primarily shifts early morning on Mondays and late afternoon on Fridays.

In addition, I make sure I am getting my personal projects done in between my work hours or on breaks. Maybe I need to walk my dog or do some laundry, so I make sure that I take time to do that for myself as well. Being able to effectively utilize my time to do my personal projects and work projects makes me happier and healthier. I don't feel guilty for neglecting my dog for work, because I can take a five-minute break to play with him or walk him during the day.

Don't feel guilty for utilizing the flexibility, because at the end of the day working from home, according to studies, means that you are probably being more efficient and effective then when you were working from the office. Enjoy the flexibility and use it wisely.

I have also found it is imperative to physically leave my work space during the day for breaks or to grab snacks and coffee. the actual act of getting up from my designated work area helps me to reboot and get more energy. The change of scenery also resets my mind and gives my eyes a rest from my computer screen.

In addition to leaving your space, you should also change your view during the working day. If you are able to switch rooms or switch windows you are looking out of that is best. But the simple change of moving from the chair to the couch or looking out of the left window and then switching to looking out the right window can totally change your work environment. I do this frequently throughout the day and go to my porch to work then my room or my office. Switching up my view throughout the day seems to make the work hours go more quickly and helps me focus.

Another guest on my podcast, Sandy Zinn, talked about how working from home is all about balance. He quoted the Karate Kid and Mr. Miyagi.

- **It Is All About Balance**. "The lesson is not just for karate only. The lesson is for the whole life. If your whole life has balance, everything will be better."

  For Sandy, he makes sure that if he is working then during that time he doesn't do personal things, but conversely when he is doing personal things, he doesn't work. When he is on a work call or sorting through work emails, he doesn't browse social media or check his personal emails. However, when he is taking a break from work, he is all in on his personal time and doesn't answer work emails or calls. He sometimes doesn't even bring his phone with him when he takes lunch and walks his dog.

- **Take Breaks.** He is also a big proponent of taking long breaks as opposed to short breaks. For him, he takes his full hour for lunch and walks his dog and gets out of the house. Instead of a bunch of small breaks here or there he will take 30 minutes or an hour a few times throughout his work day to recharge and unwind. Although that might not be feasible for everyone, he understands the value of balance.

  We have a tendency to believe that since we are working from home we have to be glued to our work "just in case" a big project or email comes to us.

While you need to be communicative, you can still take your lunch breaks and do a little laundry throughout your breaks. Don't feel guilty for taking your dog on a five minute walk or watching Netflix on your lunch break.

I am someone who likes to take small breaks here and there to let my mind rest. A five minute break to walk outside or sit in the sun always recharges me. However, you have to find what works best for you whether that is short or long breaks throughout the day.

The point is you need to take a break, how you use it or when you take it is totally up to you. Be sure to schedule breaks as well, even if you might not need one, blocking out time on your schedule for breaks is important.

- **Block Your Time.** Time-blocking is a skill that helps people organize their day and allows colleagues and even family members to see your day laid out. You may choose to share the schedule with your family or colleagues or only share a modified schedule with them. However, you should definitely schedule out the day and block off times for meetings, breaks, food, phone calls, work projects etc.

  When you physically block off time on your calendar, whether digitally or by actually writing it out, you can more clearly stick to your schedule and decline meetings or calls that interfere with that schedule. This isn't going to be a silver bullet for everyone, but it has the ability to tremendously help. You won't feel guilty for scheduling a meeting at a different time because you can actually say you already have something on your calendar for that time period. This is helpful for me when I am getting multiple requests for calls or meetings, because it keeps everything organized and cohesive.

- **Get Moving.** Taking a break to exercise is extremely important for me. Studies show that exercise and moving around helps aid in concentration, memory, and creative thinking[14]. I take 30 minutes four days during the work week to workout and I always feel refreshed afterwards.

  You can do a full workout session before or after work or right in the middle of the day. If you don't have the ability to take a full workout break, then at least get up and walk around your apartment or block. If you are stuck on a work project and can't seem to figure it out then moving around could be exactly what you need to aid in your breakthrough.

  It is helpful to actually set timers to remind you to move. Some people set these on their workout aids and watches, but I use the app Strides on my phone and reminders will pop up on my phone three times during the work day to alert me that I need to go outside and walk. These alerts have saved me time and again from being glued to my chair for hours on end.

- **Food & Water.** Listen, this sounds basic, but you would be surprised at how many people forget to

---

[14] https://www.apa.org/pubs/journals/releases/xlm-a0036577.pdf

drink enough water or eat enough food when they are working from home. You might forget because you don't have that coworker popping into your office asking you to grab lunch.

Keeping your water and food intake up is key to maintaining focus and a healthy lifestyle. However, sometimes at home we grab junk food because it is so easy and our waistline suffers (quarantine 15 anyone?). Be sure to have some healthy and easily accessible snacks in your workspace. I like to keep multiple glasses of water at my various work stations and when they are empty, I have a built-in work break. Keeping the healthy snacks within reaching distance also helps me avoid the "stand in front of the fridge" break.

Now that you have some tips and tricks to help you on your way, let's talk about how to maintain focus and concentration when you are at home. There are bound to be distractions at home whether you live alone or not. However, don't fear because you aren't the first person to deal with distraction and there are some great techniques and technologies to help you through it.

Chapter 7: How to Maintain Hyper Focus at Home

If you are new to working from home or just need some additional tools to keep you on track, then there are some great technologies to help you along your way.

- **SelfControl & Cold Turkey.** These technologies help you block sites that might distract you during the work day. Can't concentrate because you want to check your social media notifications or you have to check your personal email? Then block those distractions using these technologies. You can pick huge chunks of time or bursts of time here or there to block them. However, be sure you actually want to block them during that time because you cannot get back into them until the designated time is up.

- **Time trackers.** Keeping track of your time and taking proper breaks is key. If you aren't great at doing this yourself or want to make sure you stay on task then using a time tracking app like Toggl could help you. They have desktop and phone interfaces and even have idle time notifications.

  Their website says it best, "The Toggl Button and Toggl Desktop apps remind you when you're not tracking. Forgot to stop the timer? Toggl detects idle time and lets you decide what to do with it later."

- **Productivity Sprints.** Productivity can be hard to achieve anywhere, but especially at home when there are so many potential distractions coming at you from all directions. That's where productivity sprints can come into play and can be a game changer for you.

There are many different techniques to do this, but the most popular it seems is call the Pomodoro Technique[15]. Pomodoro means tomato in Italian and any technique that incorporates food is something I will embrace.

This technique harnesses the power of uninterrupted focus to enhance productivity. You can tweak this system to best suit your needs and make your sprints shorter or longer depending on your preferences and tasks. The generic version of this technique consists of 6 techniques as per their website:

    1. Choose a task you'd like to get done. This can be big or small, but it is something that needs your full attention.

    2. Set the Pomodoro (timer) for 25 minutes. Now you don't have to buy the special timer shaped like a tomato for this step. The gist of the idea here is any timer will do even your phone, but don't be tempted to check your phone during the sprint. Put the phone on silent and out of reach.

    3. Work on the task until your timer goes off. Since it is only 25 minutes, there will be nothing that arises that will need you to take your focus

---

[15] https://francescocirillo.com/pages/pomodoro-technique

away from the task at hand. Okay, if there is a fire or something that is a real emergency then please go attend to that and don't be a martyr to the timer. If you do get distracted by a task that isn't urgent, but nonetheless needs to get done, then write it down on a piece of paper and get back to the task at hand.

4. When the timer rings, put a checkmark on a paper. You have completed your first sprint and you will feel quite accomplished and perhaps a bit mentally drained.

5. Take a short break. Do something not work related for a short bit of time. This is where you leave the space, fill up your water bottle, take your dog on a walk, stand in the sun, or whatever you want to do to recharge your brain.

6. For every four productivity sprints, you take a longer break. This can be a 20 or 30 minute break or even longer if that's what your brain needs to rest and digest the information you just worked on.

- **Mindfulness.** In my life and profession, anxiety has been something I have struggled with since I was young. In gymnastics anxiety was always creeping into my mind and I thought I had to find ways to tamp it down which usually produced even more anxiety.

  However, the idea of mindfulness doesn't force you to "fix" the problems you face, but instead learn how to live with them or to acknowledge their existence and then move on without judgement.

As the headspace app explains, "Meditation isn't about becoming a different person, a new person, or even a better person. It's about training in awareness and getting a healthy sense of perspective. You're not trying to turn off your thoughts or feelings. You're learning to observe them without judgment. And eventually, you may start to better understand them as well."

Once I came to the realization that I didn't have to stop all negative thoughts and feelings from arising, which is impossible by the way, but rather was able to acknowledge them and move on, my peace increased dramatically and stress levels went down.

One technique in mindful meditation that helped me immeasurably is the concept of Noting[16]. The founder of headspace, Andy Puddicombe, wrote about what the technique is and how to use it.

"To begin with, it is important to use noting sparingly in the practice. We do not need to note every single thought or feeling, but simply notice when we are caught up in something so completely that we have lost our awareness of the breath or whatever the object of meditation might be. In that moment of awareness, the moment we realize we've been distracted, we use the noting to create a bit of space, as a way of letting go, and to gain some

---

[16] https://www.headspace.com/blog/2017/07/18/noting-technique-take-advantage/

clarity and learn more about our habits, tendencies, and conditioning. We don't need to think about any of this in the practice itself. It all happens very naturally."

Essentially with the concept of noting, you notice when you have become distracted from the task and you label the distraction in your mind gently as either thinking or feeling. If you are in the middle of a productivity sprint and your mind is starting to wander, you can physically or mentally write down the distraction and label it as thinking or feeling. If you are experiencing anxiety then you would note it as a feeling in your mind gently without judgement and then you would go back to your work.

This can be done during actual meditations if you decide to start a meditation practice or during your every day life. You can use this when you are taking breaks from work or focusing on your personal tasks. It is a way to note distraction and acknowledge it without judgment and then move on. This helps me every day and Andy describes it as a very soft task like brushing a feather onto a glass. It is subtle and kind with very little effort associated with it.

Sometimes we judge ourselves too harshly when we get distracted, but that is completely natural. If we never got distracted then we would never be able to slam on the brakes during our drive when we notice a child running into the road. The point when distractions become all encompassing and affect our ability to complete tasks is when distractions should be addressed. Noting sounds like a simple technique and it can be, but as humans we always seem to make things more complicated. The more you work on Noting and acknowledging distractions in a non judgmental way, the better you will become at it.

- **Put Your Phone Away.** In this day and age we have a lot of distractions, but our cell phones are by far one of the biggest. I already hear you saying, "But Alex, I do work on my phone for my job." And I would tell you that more than likely a huge majority of the time you actually spend on your phone is answering texts and checking social media that has actually nothing to do with your work life. I am generalizing here, but the fact remains a lot of people don't realize how often they are scrolling on their phone for no real reason.

  For this reason, I will actually put my phone out of my sight, face down, and turn the ringer off while I am deep in work mode. This little step yields huge results for me. It keeps me from being distracted by social media notifications or spam phone calls. If you want to be really sneaky with yourself then put it on airplane mode or sleep mode so the notifications don't even pop up.

  Even though I use my cell phone for work, there is almost nothing that comes directly to my phone that isn't also connected to my work email. You can set up your email system, or your IT person can, to where you get all voicemails as emails. This has helped me so much when I am in the zone and don't want to be distracted by phone calls. If something is urgent or important then the person will be leaving a voicemail or following up with an email so then I will be notified and can follow-up with them.

If you don't believe this can work for you then track your phone time. On iPhones you can head to Settings and find Screen Time. When you turn this on it tracks where you spend your time on your phone including specifically how many times you pick up your phone in a day. It is honestly eye opening to see where your time goes. You can even set app limits, downtime, and more.

Once you see where your time is being spent on your phone, you might be able to better schedule your use of your phone during the work day. For me, I realized I was spending a lot of time on apps and picking up my phone for literally no reason. The tracking showed me when I picked up my phone and took an action and when I picked up my phone because of habit and no action ensued from the pick up.

- **Self Care.** Even with these suggestions on maintaining focus, there will be days when you don't feel like you did a great job. That is bound to happen and the most important part of the process is not judging yourself for it.

Acknowledge that your To Do list was left undone or that your kids needed you to "help them" a million time in the day. But whatever you do, don't judge yourself for those things. Working from home requires you to be a real human being and not a robot. As being a human in the workplace becomes normalized, which it slowly is, the less you will have the guilt or shame for taking time to be human during the work day.

Practicing this type of humanity is a form of self care and it is vitally important in your life. It becomes even more important when you live and work in the same place. If you aren't taking the time out of your day to disconnect from work and take time for yourself then you will not be a productive employee or human being. Things will start to slip and anxiety and stress will begin to take over.

Allow some time for yourself throughout the day, every day and learn what works for you.

Finding the techniques and tricks that help you maintain a work life and personal life that you love is the key. There is no one-size fits all working from home guide or style. You get to walk through a buffet of choices and pick the exact style you want for yourself. You are essentially curating a gallery of art with the pieces that make you most happy. It doesn't matter if the art experts say you hung the pieces in the wrong place, it is a gallery for YOU so it only matters how it works for you.

Chapter 8: Takeaways

You now have a toolbox of tips and tricks to help you work from home in a new way. Using these strategies and modifying them for your own lifestyle is the key to creating a remote work life that truly works for you, your job, and your family.

10 Things to Remember About Working From Home

1. **It is all about balance.**
2. **Utilize the flexibility.**
3. **Get Hygge in your office and home.**
4. **Communicate effectively and often with work and family.**
5. **Create a routine and stick to it.**
6. **Move your body and take breaks.**
7. **Set boundaries for yourself and others.**
8. **Give yourself grace and be mindful of distractions.**
9. **Prioritize Self Care.**
10. **Create a plan that fits with your life. There is no one-size fits all.**

I hope you enjoyed this book, be sure to listen to episodes 5-8 of my podcast, **Your Potential for Everything**. Episodes 5-8 is a series on Working From Home and I interview guests about their journey to the remote-work lifestyle and their tips and tricks to being successful. Be sure to purchase my next book in the series, **The Multipotentialite's Guide to Side Hustles and Entrepreneurship**. And if you haven't already, purchase a copy of the first book in the series, **The Multipotentialite's Guide to Networking in the Virtual Age**.

Chapter 9: Resources

My podcast: Your Potential For Everything -
http://yourpotentialforeverything.libsyn.com/
website
Maybe you don't have one true calling. Perhaps you are a renaissance woman or a jack of all trades like Maya Angelou or Aristotle. On Your Potential for Everything you will learn from multipotentialites about their unique abilities to jump across industries and be successful in seemingly disparate fields. New episode drop every Tuesday and you can listen and subscribe wherever you get your podcasts. Be sure to leave a review!

The Multipotentialite's Guide: Networking In The Virtual Age: Learn How to Network, Make Lasting Connections, and Land a Job In the Digital Age -
https://amzn.to/2ClmU26
This is the first book in The Multipotentialite's Guide series and it is all about helping you network, connect, and land a job in the digital age. Benefit from my experience and ability to easily explain the ins and outs of a variety of topics. Be sure to leave a review!

The Bone-Handled Stiletto - https://amzn.to/
2Ovjtbo
This story tracks the Bumpalino family from Lercara Friddi Sicily to Newark, New Jersey. The story follows the lives of Fortunado, Giuseppina, Nicky, Concetta, Don Moterano, and Rocco through their assimilation into American culture. It is a look at the Mafia and the beginnings of the RICO laws and witness protection

and how it applied. This book has intrigue, crime, violence, undercover police work, and much more.

The Year of Living Danishly - https://bit.ly/ 2OH6oMh
When she was suddenly given the opportunity of a new life in rural Jutland, journalist and archetypal Londoner Helen Russell discovered a startling statistic: the happiest place on earth isn't Disneyland, but Denmark, a land often thought of by foreigners as consisting entirely of long dark winters, cured herring, Lego and pastries.

Headspace - https://www.headspace.com/Meditation isn't about becoming a different person, a new person, or even a better person. It's about training in awareness and getting a healthy sense of perspective. You're not trying to turn off your thoughts or feelings. You're learning to observe them without judgment. And eventually, you may start to better understand them as well.

Slack - https://slack.com/
With channels in Slack, you and your team know where to go to ask questions, share updates and stay in the loop.

Pomodoro Technique - https://francescocirillo.com/ pages/pomodoro-technique
For many people, time is an enemy. We race against the clock to finish assignments and meet deadlines. The Pomodoro Technique teaches you to work with time, instead of struggling against it. A revolutionary time management system, it is at once deceptively simple to learn and life-changing to use.

The Book Club for Professionals Who Don't Read Good - https://bit.ly/2DL39Bz
We focus on purchasing books from minority-owned shops and/or donating to nonprofits and charities. We also emphasize reading books written by members of our book club community.

Zoom - https://zoom.us/
A web-based video conferencing tool with a local, desktop client and a mobile app that allows users to meet online, with or without video. Zoom users can choose to record sessions, collaborate on projects, and share or annotate on one another's screens, all with one easy-to-use platform.

Esports Trade Association - https://esportsta.org/membership/
The ESTA promotes, protects, and advances the broader interests of the esports community.

Made in United States
Orlando, FL
23 February 2025